OUR WORLD IN COLOUR
CANADA

OUR
WORLD IN
COLOUR
CANADA

Photography by Ken Straiton
Text by Isobel Nanton

The Guidebook Company Limited

Distributors

Australia and New Zealand: The Book Company,
100 Old Pittwater Road, Brookvale, NSW 2100, Australia.

Canada: Prentice Hall Canada,
1870 Birchmount Road, Scarborough, Ontario MIP 257,
Canada.

Hong Kong: China Guides Distribution Services Ltd.,
14 Ground Floor, Lower Kai Yuen Lane, North Point, Hong Kong.

India and Nepal: UBS Publishers' Distributors Ltd.,
5 Ansari Road, Post Box 7015, New Delhi 110 002, India.

Singapore and Malaysia: MPH Distributors (S) PTE Ltd.,
601 Sims Drive, No. 03/07-21, Pan-I Complex, Singapore 1438.

UK: Springfield Books Limited,
Springfield House, Norman Road, Dendy Dale,
Huddersfield HD8 8TH, West Yorkshire, England.

USA: Publishers Group West Inc.,
4065 Hollis, Emeryville, CA 94608, USA.

Text and captions by Isobel Nanton

Photography by Ken Straiton

Edited by Lesley Clark and Ralph Kiggell
An A to Z of Fun Facts by Mary Cooch

Designed by Joan Law Design & Photography
Colour separations by Rainbow Graphic Arts Co., Ltd.
Printed in Hong Kong
by Toppan Printing Company (HK) Limited

ISBN 962-217-103-6

Title spread
Canada is the world's sixth-largest producer of wheat. Here a thresher works geometric patterns on a field of hard red spring wheat, used for bread, outside Regina, Saskatchewan — a province which alone grows 60 percent of Canada's wheat.

Right
The ochres, greens, yellows and reds of autumn are epitomized in the wild and beautiful forests of Forillon National Park, on the outer tip of the Gaspe Peninsula, Quebec. Traditionally summer hunting and fishing grounds for the Micmac Indians, Forillon's boreal forest and high limestone-cliffed coastline now lure many an autumn visitor to view the leaves.

Pages 6–7
One of the former settlements of immigrant Acadians, Lunenberg, Nova Scotia, is now base for Atlantic Canada's largest processing plant and fleet of deep-sea trawlers. From here trawlers head out to fish the Grand Banks of Newfoundland. Among the church spires are two venerable buildings — Presbyterian St Andrew's (1754) and Anglican St John's (1753).

Pages 8–9
As dawn comes up on the Lillooet River, near Mt Currie Indian Reservation, British Columbia, the water gleams under that luminescent light unique to the Pacific Northwest. From here the river meanders through the rich Pemberton Valley potato-growing area, before emptying into Lillooet Lake.

Pages 10–11
Since 1954 the residents of Quebec City have held their annual Winter Carnival every February to celebrate ice and snow in all their forms. Snow palaces dwarf intrepid snow bathers participating in Le Bain de Neige (snowbath) ritual, encouraged by Bonhomme de neige (snowman), the carnival's official mascot.

Pages 12–13
Thrusting skywards the Canadian National (CN) Tower in Toronto, the nation's most populous city, epitomizes the energy and ambition radiating from Canada's financial hub. Here the downtown skyscrapers overlook Lake Ontario and Centre and Ward Islands, pockets of tranquility mere minutes away from the action.

fifth of the whole of Canada and, like Ontario, is almost absurdly blessed with resources. Most of the world's asbestos and a great deal of its pulp and paper come from here, while Montreal is, arguably, the cultural pulse of the country. Thoughts on art, music and theatre are exchanged between natives of Quebec sipping *café au lait* on the Rue St Denis. The annual Montreal 'Just for Laughs' Comedy Festival is the biggest of its kind in the world.

New Quebec, innovative city of intellectuals and contemporary culture, goes hand in hand with the old. Frontenac lords it over the St Lawrence, which abuts the Plains of Abraham. Here General Wolfe defeated Montcalm and today, the famous heroic Vingt-doux Regiment still make the city their headquarters. Quebec City exudes tradition, and is thus an anomaly in the heart of ever-changing North America.

To sense the earthy side of Quebec's character, spend some time at a place in the countryside, such as the Gaspe Peninsula. A pastoral idyll, the Gaspe lies deep in the heart of Catholic rural French Canada. Like scenes from a 19th-century novel, families work the fields together and milk cows by hand at the roadside in the twilight.

Sights of a different kind can be seen over Bonaventure Island and neighbouring Perce Rock, for this is the premier sight in North America for ornithologists. Here, avid bird-watchers view flocks of cormorants, great black-backed gulls, herring gulls, kittiwakes, razorbill auks, puffins, petrels, and over 50,000 white gannets whose individual wing spans stretch over two metres (six feet).

Bordering Quebec to the east lie the provinces collectively known as the Maritimes. Tide-watchers flock to New Brunswick to view the advancing and receding waters of the Bay of Fundy. Spring attracts harvesters who comb the moist banks of the St John River for the first fronds of the fiddlehead, an ostrich fern which resembles the curled head of a violin. In season, these great Canadian delicacies grace gourmet plates from Victoria to Bonaventure.

Neighbouring Nova Scotia has been home to sailors and fishermen for generations. During the Second World War, corvettes and destroyers from the Royal Canadian Navy surged out from Halifax to protect merchant convoys from Nazi U-boat attack. Boats skirt around Sable Island, off Nova Scotia. Known as the Graveyard of the Atlantic, Sable's 32-kilometre (20-mile) shifting crescent of dune and beach has shipwrecked 200 vessels in the past 170 years and is still considered a major navigational hazard.

On land, Nova Scotia's shore stretches from Peggy's Cove to Lunenburg and Blue Rocks. Studded with white summer-houses, excellent inns and seafood restaurants bulging with Malpeque Bay oysters, the run vies with the Banff-Jasper Highway for the title of the most scenic drive in Canada.

Prince Edward Island (PEI), Canada's smallest province, is Nova Scotia's neighbour. The island lies crescent-shaped off the coast of New Brunswick in the Gulf of St Lawrence. At no point are you ever more than 16 kilometres (ten miles) from the ocean, but though PEI is small in size, it is big in soul.

The Micmac Indians called her Abegweit — 'cradle in the waves'. Lucy Maud Montgomery set her classic tale *Anne of Green Gables* in this miniature paradise with its icey-blue waters, golden beaches and red sandstone cliffs.

Five million Malpeque oysters are harvested each year from PEI's north shores. Atlantic storms regularly churn up Irish moss, the purplish seaweed that grows on the ocean floor, and deposit it on the island's shores. Half the world's carageenin, an emulsifier, is derived from this harvest. The 20,000 hectares (50,000 acres) of land cultivated for potatoes have gained PEI the nickname 'Spud Island'. But for the thriving tourist industry inspired by Lucy Montgomery's work, the island remains a haven of peace. There are many who would agree with one writer's words:

Once predominantly a Christian country, Canada's religious denominations now encompass Christianity, Judaism, Buddhism, Sikhism, Hinduism and Islam. Here churches provide some of the prettiest sights in the country. Greenock Church (1824), St Andrews, New Brunswick (top left). *Brigus on Conception Bay, Newfoundland* (centre left). *Tadoussac Church (1647) located at the confluence of Saguenay and St Lawrence Rivers, northeast of Quebec City, is one of the oldest wooden chapels in North America* (lower left). *Ukrainian church near Beausejour, Manitoba* (top). *Provincial churchyard south shore, Quebec* (above).

Peace! You never know what peace is until you walk on the shores or in the fields or along the winding red roads of Prince Edward Island in a summer twilight when the dew is falling and the old old stars are peeping out and the sea keeps its mighty tryst with the little land it loves. You find your soul then. You realize that youth is not a vanished thing but something that dwells forever in the heart.

From the smallest province, Prince Edward Island, we move to Newfoundland, the oldest. Strong evidence suggests that Labrador is the only land left on the surface of the earth today which actually existed when the earth was formed. It is the closest part of Canada to Europe and Vikings settled here around the year AD 1000. From time immemorial, devastating Atlantic storms have battered this ancient rock, breeding 'a hardiness into its inhabitants, a toughness not duplicated even in the survivors of the Depression on the prairies.'

The size of Ireland and the fourth-largest island in Canada, Newfoundland has a unique culture. 'Newfies' brew their own beer, make their own music and view the world with a delightfully obstreperous irony, peculiarly their own.

North towards Alaska from the Maritimes stretch the Northwest Territories which occupy more than one-third of Canada, much of it in the Arctic. It is the land of the magnificent aurora borealis, of the midnight sun and of 24-hour summer days.

The 80,000 Inuit residents of the north live in times of great transition as world mores on hunting dictate changes in their ancient life-style. Their soapstone carvings still fetch high prices at galleries but demand has fallen off for animal pelts and, gradually, the territories turn to tourism as a viable economic alternative.

Outsiders travel to such towns as Tuktoyaktuk, meaning 'looks like a caribou' to view the 'pingos'. Situated on the shore of the Beaufort Sea, 160 kilometres (100 miles) south of the Arctic Ocean's permanent polar ice-cap, the pingos are giant boils with solid cores of ice that erupt from the earth and gradually become covered with soil and vegetation.

To the west the last, but not least, of this collection of Canadian territories is the Yukon, beloved of Canada's best-known bard — Robert Service. Entranced by this huge country of 'big dizzy mountains' and 'deep deathline valleys', Service devoted his writings to this land of the Yu-kunah, Loucheux for 'great river'. Echoing the feelings of many a Canadian immigrant, Service wrote: 'The freshness, the freedom, the fairness — O God! How I'm stuck on it all.'

The province he made his own stretches from the British Columbian forests to the Arctic coast of the Beaufort Sea. The high ice-fields of the main park, Kluane, are, as the park manual states, 'one of the truest wilderness areas remaining in the world today.' Kluane's ice-fields include five of the longest glaciers outside the polar regions, Canada's highest mountain, Mount Logan, nearly 6,000 metres (20,000 feet) above sea level, and at least 12 other peaks over 4,500 metres (15,000 feet).

Though Service wrote his most famous lines about the Yukon, they serve as a coda to the whole vast country of Canada, and as a panegyric to that most striking of Canadian experiences — winter:

The winter! the brightness that blinds you
The white land locked tight as a drum,
The cold fear that follows and finds you,
The silence that bludgeons you dumb.
The snows that are older than history,
The woods where the weird shadows slant;
The stillness, the moonlight, the mystery,
I've bade 'em good-bye — but I can't.

Quebec City's official mascot at the winter carnival (top). *Frozen Montmorency Falls* (centre). *Decorated canoes front Lake Louise and the famous Chateau Lake Louise* (above). *Long Beach, on the west coast of Vancouver Island* (right).

Above
*Backed by the Northshore
Mountains, office blocks in
downtown Vancouver glow at
dusk. The Lions, the twin
mountain peaks which rise here
above Burrard Inlet were
known in Indian legend as the
'Chief's daughters' or 'sisters'.
They keep watch over the peace
and brotherhood of the Pacific
coast, 'wrapped in the suns, the
snows and the stars of all the
seasons' wrote Canadian poet
Pauline Johnson.*

Right
*Autumn frosts turn the leaves
on the trees of a typical avenue
in Vancouver's Point Grey
residential district.*

Left
*The northwest coast native
Indians had the richest cultural
heritage in the country. Their
intricately carved totem poles
incorporated their tribal crests,
depicting such creatures as
beaver, bear, wolf, shark, raven,
whale, eagle and frog. Carved of
malleable red cedar, the totems
were used as memorial poles,
house posts and ceremonial
icons.*

23

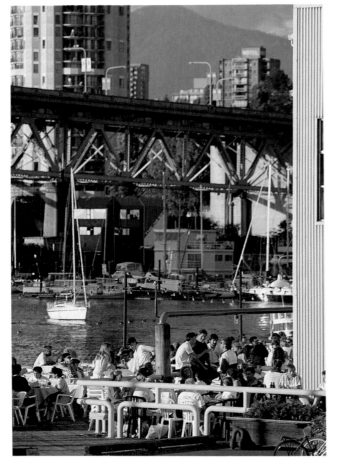

Left
*Once a derelict railway
terminus for a few defunct
lines, Granville Island, where
this restaurant is situated was
restored and opened in 1979.
The Island is the place to shop
in Vancouver for fresh produce,
smoked salmon, wild rice,
maple syrup and other
Canadian delicacies. Theatres,
restaurants and galleries, many
of them garnering architectural
awards, round out this now-
thriving area.*

Above
*One of the perpetually liveliest
parts of downtown Vancouver,
Chinatown is the second-
biggest Chinese urban area on
the continent after San
Francisco. Fresh vegetables
from the Fraser Valley, exotic
fruits from the Far East and
fragrant Peking Duck —
Chinatown stocks them all,
making it not just a tourist
attraction but a focal shopping
point too.*

Above
Alfresco lunch at Bridges Restaurant on Granville Island is the choice of yachties who can berth nearby, business people who can ride over from downtown by water taxi, and casual visitors who enjoy the restaurant's west-coast cuisine.

Right
Converted tugboats, which are still used on Vancouver's Fraser River to nudge log booms into place, here double as water taxis to ferry passengers across False Creek, to and from Granville Island.

Above
Since 1886 all basic training of Royal Canadian Mounted Police (RCMP) recruits has taken place at the Depot Division in Regina. More than 20,000 RCMP work across the country. Here in formal dress gear they symbolize the law-abiding north, carrying on the legacy of the original Northwest Mounted Police. Initial training at the police college consists of an intensive six-month course.

Left
The majority of North American cities are laid out on a grid system and downtown Regina, the capital of Saskatchewan is no exception. In the foreground the Parliament Buildings oversee business in this city of 186,521 people. In the distance stretch mile after mile after mile of prairie grain fields, the lifeblood of the Saskatchewan economy.

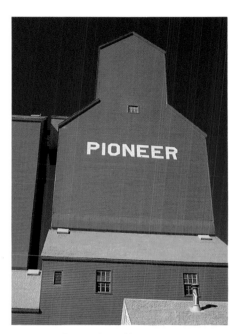

Many residents of small prairie towns like to joke that if you blink when you drive past, you will miss their town. Here, typically, the highway splits to bypass the community of Richardson, near Regina. Flat grain fields stretch as far as the eye can see and primary-coloured grain elevators store the grain until it can be shipped to either coast by rail. The Saskatchewan Wheat pool is Canada's largest grain-handling company.

Saskatoon (above three), the largest city in Saskatchewan, still exudes a pioneer, small-town spirit and is renowned for its hospitality. A well-kept barn on the Saskatchewan prairie symbolizes the same pioneer spirit (left). Closing the truck door on a good harvest of rapeseed, a prairie farmer near Rosthern, Saskatchewan, may well head south, with other 'snowbirds', to warmer climes when winter comes (right).

Left
Batoche National Historic Site, 44 kilometres (27 miles) southwest of Prince Albert, Saskatchewan, is the site of a former Metis (mixed blood) community and the scene of a major confrontation in 1885 during the Northwest Rebellion. After the clash, Louis Riel, Metis leader, surrendered, was tried and hung. The church and rectory are all that remain from 1885.

Above
Neon grain stooks and grain elevator welcome the traveller to the prairie town of Rosthern, Saskatchewan. Communities across the three prairie provinces of Alberta, Manitoba and Saskatchewan are famous for their warm hospitality and generous acceptance of strangers.

Though the era of steam trains is long gone, certain belching locomotives across the country recall a time when iron rails opened up the nation. The Royal Hudson (above) travels up the coast daily from Vancouver. The Prairie Dog Central Village Train (left) thunders towards Winnipeg, Manitoba.

Above
Over 100,000 Mennonites call Canada home and this heritage village at Steinbach, Manitoba recaptures their homesteading history. Mennonites, Hutterites, Amish and Doukhobors left religious intolerance in Europe to settle in North America in the 19th century, seeking peace and tolerance. Hard-working and successful farmers, Mennonites live in the community which is their congregation.

Right
The Steinbach Livery Restaurant menu features Mennonite specialities, using produce grown on the communal farms. In Alberta, prairie townfolk regularly shop at the Hutterite colonies for fresh corn and other produce.

Tasty Traditional Dishes

Platz
TRADITIONAL DESSERT, FRESHLY BAKED RHUBARD AND SUGAR SQUARES.

Pluma Moos
TRADITIONAL MENNONITE FRUIT DISH, MADE FROM SEVERAL DIFFERENT DRIED FRUITS AND CREAM.

Vareniki
BOILED POCKETS OF SOFT DOUGH, FILLED WITH COTTAGE CHEESE. SERVED WITH CREAM GRAVY.

Farmer Sausage
PORK SAUSAGE, LIGHTLY SEASONED, SMOKED AND FRIED, IN THE TRADITIONAL MANNER.

Bread
BAKED FROM STONE-GROUND FLOUR, MILLED IN THE MUSEUM'S WIND DRIVEN GRIST MILL.

Borscht
MADE FROM HEARTY BEEF STOCK, TENDER GREEN CABBAGE, ONIONS AND GARDEN POTATOES.

LIVERY
RESTAU
RESTAU
HOU
MONDAY
10 A.M.
SUN.
12 NOON

Until the building of the Panama Canal, Winnipeg was the major city of Western Canada. Once the Pacific Ocean became accessible through the port of Vancouver, Winnipeg lost some status but still commerce as evidenced by the Portage Place Complex in the heart of the downtown area.

Above

The French community of Winnipeg is one of the largest French Canadian communities outside of Quebec and the St Boniface Basilica a major religious symbol. It was rebuilt following a disastrous fire in 1968.

Right

The Manitoba Legislative Buildings, Winnipeg, form a popular backdrop for wedding parties. A four-metre (13-foot) -high statue called Golden Boy tops the buildings. A symbol of the prairies, the young runner carries a sheaf of grain and holds aloft a torch.

Lower Fort Garry built during the 1830s. Winnipeg, 30 kilometres (18 miles) down the Red River from Fort Garry, served as the Hudson's Bay Company's administration centre for the vast fur tracts of Rupert's Land. This National Historic Sight has preserved the fur loft (now doubled as a saleshop) (left), the farm manager's house (above) and a blacksmith's (right).

The vastness of the Yukon Territory
encompasses mighty rivers, lakes,
mountains and not, incidentally the best
fishing in Canada. A bridge spans Miles
Canyon near the major city of Whitehorse
(left). Travellers scan the crystal-clear
waters at a campground near Haines
Junction, headquarters of Kluane National
Park (above). Located at the junction of the
Alaska Highway and Haine Highway, the
park is a stop off on the famous Alaska
Highway, built between 1942 and 1945 by
US Army corps. A successful angler
displays his salmon catch near Dalton
Post, Yukon Territory (right).

The Klondike Gold Rush of
1897–8 to the Yukon remains
the most famous of Canada's
many gold rushes. Here the
Frantic Follies Vaudeville
Revue in Whitehorse evokes
those maverick days when 60
steamboats were in active
service plying the Yukon River,
in an era when the mother lode
delivered over US$50 million of
gold.

Above
All roads lead to Hog Town. Highway 401, the main artery of Toronto snakes past Lake Ontario, with an endless stream of traffic.

Right
Restaurants proliferate on King Street West, Toronto, to service patrons of the Royal Alexander Theatre and hungry business people.

*Like all major centres in transition,
Toronto contains in its precincts the ultra-
modern and the old. Gothic superimposed
on the glass façades of the highest-priced
real estate in the country.*

Below
While Toronto prides itself on bustle and hustle, the urban sprawl is contained by Lake Ontario and pockets of greenery which provide tranquil areas for harried urban dwellers.

Right
Street cars transport workers who would rather not contend with Toronto's notoriously aggressive drivers. A thriving Chinatown, upmarket shopping areas and clubs: the city has them all.

Left
The greatest waterfall in the world by volume, Niagara Falls, Ontario, is split by Goat Island into American and Canadian (Horseshoe) Falls. A favourite destination with North American and Oriental honeymooners, the falls can be explored by the Maid of the Mist *boat which carries sightseers to the foot of the falls to watch the flow of water — about 155 million litres at any one time.*

Right
The Sparks Street Mall here reflects the seat of the Federal Government, Parliament Buildings, Ottawa. Begun in 1859 the buildings were finished in 1866, just in time for confederation in 1867 when Ottawa was named the capital city of the New Dominion. The buildings are widely considered to be Canada's best example of developed, picturesque Gothic revival style. Appropriately for the country which prides itself on its world role as an honest broker, the grand central tower is called the Peace Tower.

Above
Statues and monuments stipple Ottawa, so many in fact that many a career diplomat spending years in the city, is hard pressed to name them all. Here Jacques Cartier hails the lands of the New World.

Left
The central artery of Ottawa, the Rideau Canal reflects the lights of the Houses of Parliament and on the other bank the Chateau Laurier Hotel. In winter, politicians, support staff and visitors skate on the frozen waters of the Rideau.

Left
Old Fort Henry in Kingston, Ontario, was built during the war of 1812 to guard both the outlet to the St Lawrence River and the Kingston navy yards against American attack. Today it houses a museum of military arms and equipment. In summer the Fort Henry guard demonstrate precision drill manoeuvres.

Above
Founded in 1841, Queens University in Kingston, on Lake Ontario, is a major research university, housing one of Canada's finest university libraries in its old limestone buildings.

Above and right
In the 1950s and 1960s the St Lawrence Parks Commission developed Upper Canada Village near Morrisburg, Ontario, as a replica of a 19th-century community that might have existed along the banks of the St Lawrence River. The village includes a pioneer farm, store, doctor's house and cheese factory with all buildings authentically furnished. Guides in period costume demonstrate and explain those times and lives.

Canadian horse farms, like this one outside Aurora, Ontario, became famous in the 1960s when E P Taylor's Northern Dancer became the first Canadian-bred horse to win the Kentucky Derby in 1964. His record of two minutes flat for the one and a quarter miles has only ever been bettered by Secretariat. Retired to stud, Northern Dancer became the cornerstone of Mr Taylor's breeding empire — the most successful in the world.

Glimpses of rural Ontario. Mennonite Boys in their traditional clothes in Waterloo County (above). *A still-life glance at country life in the Robertson Home (1784), Upper Canada Village* (right).

Above
Muskoka cottage country, a picturesque recreation area east of Georgian Bay. Autumn colours evoke the palettes of some of the Group of Seven, Canada's best-known painters.

Left
An 80-kilometre (50-mile) section of the St Lawrence River extending downstream from Lake Ontario encompasses the 1000 Islands area of the St Lawrence Seaway. The islands were once favourite camping grounds of the Iroquois.

Below
The regal Chateau Frontenac dominates this section of the frozen St Lawrence River and to the west the Plains of Abraham, Quebec City. Here a crucial battle was fought during the Seven Year War, on 13 September 1759, when General Wolfe's vastly outnumbered army scaled the cliffs below the chateau site and routed the French camp of General Montcalm. Both generals were mortally wounded in the battle.

Above
Contemporary Quebecois and many visitors from the rest of Canada and the United States converge on frozen Quebec City in February for the annual carnival, replete with snow palaces and friendly bonhommes!

The charm of Quebec City draws visitors back time and again to this corner of Europe in the heart of North America. Horse-drawn carriages are the most popular transport for visitors in winter and summer (left); delicate ice sculptures please the eye (above) and the city literally bulges with fine accommodation and superb places to eat (right).

Left
The Petit Champlain area of Quebec City is another gourmet destination. Specialities of the area include tourtière *(a spicy meat pie) and maple syrup concoctions.*

Above
As the low evening light of winter settles across the Place d'Armes, several more months will pass before the sap starts to run in the trees, transforming their sombre silhouettes into a more convivial meeting place.

Between 1783 and 1784 waves of loyalists landed at such places as this — Loyalist Landing, New Brunswick, in the Canadian Maritimes. These loyalists were American colonists who supported the British cause during the American revolution. From this spot they would have looked south across the line to the changing face of the New World.

Above
The Market Slip leads up to Saint John, major industrial hub of the maritime province of New Brunswick.

Right
Forest covers 90 percent of the province of New Brunswick, so timber dominates the economy, providing fuel for pulp and paper mills. Pulp consumes 80 percent of the timber harvested.

*Fishing off the Grand Banks of
Newfoundland remains the main
economic buttress of this North Atlantic
island as witnessed by the seagulls at
Cappahayden Harbour. The rural feel of
such communities as this near Clarenville,
evokes memories of Ireland, from which
many Newfoundland immigrants escaped
during the Potato Famine.*

Following pages
*Ten species of maple are native to Canada
out of the 125 species worldwide. Sugar,
black, silver red and striped maples
predominate in Eastern Canada, hub of the
maple sugar industry, while the vine
maple dots the forests of the west coast. In
1965 the red maple leaf was confirmed as
the national symbol with the proclamation
of the Canadian flag.*

AN A TO Z OF FUN FACTS

A

Alberta Fourth largest province in Canada with an area of 661,188 km² (171,292 mi²). Alberta has a population of some 3 million people and in recent years has become wealthy from abundant oil and gas deposits.

Arctic Tundra About a quarter of Canada is barren Arctic tundra. Lakes are frozen from November to May in the south Arctic, which is the home of the Inuit people. In the north the freeze lasts from November to June and glaciers cover about 5% of the area.

B

Beavers One of the national symbols of Canada. The trade in beaver fur was thriving by the 1600s. French and British settlers traded with the Indians for beaver pelts, thus hastening the decline of the Indians' traditional way of life. The trade in beaver fur lasted almost 200 years.

British Columbia Usually known simply as BC, the province of British Columbia is 366,160 km² (948,600 mi²) with a population of some 3 million.

C

Cabot, John The Italian explorer, sailing under the British flag, reached Canada in 1497. He was searching for the (non-existent) northwest passage. He called the land 'new found land', hence the province named Newfoundland today.

Cartier, Jacques Like John Cabot, Jacques Cartier came to Canada searching for the northwest passage. He arrived in 1534 and landed on Prince Edward Island, which he named Ile Ste Jean. He sailed down the St Lawrence River and arrived at the site of present-day Montreal.

Casa Loma A castle near the centre of Toronto. Built in 1911 by Sir Henry Pellatt, an eccentric millionaire, the castle has gold-plated bathroom fixtures, private elevators and riding stables with tiled floors, mahogany stalls and porcelain troughs. Secret passageways run under the house and were used by the servants so that Sir Henry did not have to see them.

Constitution Act In 1982 the Constitution Act was passed to enable Canadians to amend their constitution without the approval of the British Parliament.

Cordillera The Canadian stretch of a mountain system running the length of the Pacific Coast of the Americas. The Cordillera covers 16% of the country. The range has distinct sub-regions: the Rocky Mountains, the Coast Mountain Range and the Inside Passage.

D

Diamond Tooth Gertie's Gambling Hall The world's northernmost casino, situated in Dawson City 240 km (150 miles) south of the Arctic Circle. Starring Gertie who leads the floor shows and the cancan dancers.

Dinosaur Provincial Park Situated in the province of Alberta, the park was set up to preserve the many dinosaur remains found there. Once a subtropical swamp, the park is now a sandstone landscape where dinosaur fossils have been preserved where they were found.

E

Ellesmere Island Near Greenland in the Arctic tundra, Ellesmere Island is home to the rare Arctic wolf (*canis lupus arctos*).

F

First inhabitants Prehistoric Asians crossed the land bridge which existed at what is now the Bering Strait some 25,000 years ago. As these people spread out across Canada, they became distinct tribal groups, with different languages and cultures. An estimated 250,000 of their descendants lived in Canada when the first Europeans arrived.

Front de Liberation du Quebec A separatist organization whose acts of terrorism in October 1970 led to the declaration of martial law for a month. The separatist movement is still strong in Quebec, despite their defeat in the 1980 referendum.

G

Great Canadian Bathtub Race In the city of Nanaimo, Vancouver Island, the bathtub race has become an annual international event. Homemade tubs cross the 56-km (35-mi) Georgia Strait to Vancouver. The first bathtubber to cross the strait and ring a brass bell is the winner.

H

Head-Smashed-In Buffalo Jump A UNESCO World Heritage Site, this is the place where for nearly 6,000 years the Plains Indians drove herds of bison over the cliffs as an efficient form of hunting.

I

Inuit One of the indigenous people of Canada. The Inuit's ancestors, and those of the other Indian peoples in Canada, crossed the land bridge which existed at the Bering Strait thousands of years ago. The Inuit are the people who remained in the Arctic, developing a different culture from the Indian tribes which moved further south. They have adapted to a remarkably harsh climate and still manage to retain much of their traditional way of life despite the encroachments of the modern world.

K

Kitchener A town in Ontario founded by German settlers in the early 19th century. Originally called Berlin, the name was changed to Kitchener because of anti-German feeling during the First World War.

Klondike Goldrush The discovery of gold in 1896 brought 80,000 people to the rivers of the Klondike in Yukon. Previously this mountainous wilderness had been inhabited only by the Dene Indians, who had lived there some 60,000 years. The rivers ran dry of gold in 1902, bringing an end to the goldrush and reducing the population of Dawson City, from 30,000 at the peak of the boom, to 1,000 in 1910 to about 600 today.

L

Lake Hazen The largest lake north of the Arctic Circle. Situated in the cold, harsh High Arctic, Lake Hazen is a geographical oddity because it is surrounded by a relatively warm valley — called a thermal oasis. Because of this, the lake is ringed by profuse vegetation and visited by abundant wildlife.

Location Canada stretches 5,500 km (3,400 mi) from the Atlantic in the East to the Pacific Ocean in the west. Ellesmere Island is the most northern point, 4,600 km (2,734 mi) from Middle Island in Lake Erie.

M

Manitoba Manitoba is named after the Indian word for 'great spirit'. The province is 650,090 km² (250,934 mi²) and has a population of over a million, half of which lives in Winnipeg.

N

New Brunswick Canada's only official bilingual province, New Brunswick is 73,437 km² (28,346 mi²) and has a population of 700,000. Its main product is paper and wood pulp

Newfoundland The fishing grounds off Newfoundland have been fished by European fishermen since the 15th century. The province is 404,520 km² (156,144 mi²) but has a population of only just over half a million. The people are mainly of British descent and speak a unique form of English based on the West Country and Irish accents of their 16th-century ancestors.

Niagara Falls 131 km (83 mi) southwest of Toronto, Lake Erie overflows into Lake Ontario, forming Niagara Falls. The water flows at 35,000 cubic litres per second and descends 56 m (186 ft). A famous Frenchman called Blondin crossed over the falls in 1859 on a tightrope. He repeated his journey several times, on stilts, turning cartwheels, stopping to cook a meal halfway and with another man on his back.

Northwest Territories One of the two territories, Northwest Territories covers nearly one-third of Canada. Larger than India, the territory is 3.3 million km² (1.3 million mi²) but has only 50,000 inhabitants. The north of the province is home to the Inuits. The south is inhabited by another Indian tribe, the Dene.

Nova Scotia 55,941 km² (21,593 mi²) with a population of just under one million. Nova Scotia was formerly called Arcadia by the French. It is still inhabited by its original people, the Micmacs, along with 77% of the population of British descent and 10% of French extraction.

O

Ontario Second largest province and most populous with nine million people, covering 1.3 million km² (0.5 million mi²). It contains one quarter of the world's fresh water in the form of numerous lakes and 400,000 rivers. It also has 80% of the world's trout fishing waters.

P

Pile 0'Bones The former name of the city of Regina in Saskatchewan. So named because the Cree Indians once dried buffalo meat and cleaned hides at the nearby Wascana Creek, leaving bones on the banks. The name was changed to Regina in honour of Queen Victoria.

Prairie Dog Central The oldest authentic steam train in operation in North America. During the summer, the train makes a daily two-hour trip to Grosse Isle, 58 km (36 mi) northwest of Winnipeg, Manitoba.

Prince Edward Island The smallest province, the island is sometimes described as two beaches divided by potato fields. It has an area of 5,657 km² (2,183 mi²) and a population of only 120,000, although it is the most densely populated province. The island was originally inhabited by the Micmac Indians and a small community still lives there, specializing in basket weaving.

Q

Quebec Canada's largest province in area, covering nearly a fifth of the country. Quebec has a population of 6.5 million, 80% of whom are French speakers. The first French explorer of Quebec was Jacques Cartier who charted the St Lawrence River in 1534–5. In 1663, the area, called New France, was proclaimed a royal colony. In 1754, the French and Indians began a nine year war over the territory which was ended by British intervention. In 1763, France ceded her interests to Britain, but the Quebec Act of 1772 allowed Quebec to retain the French language and institutions.

R

Red River Rebellion In 1869 the government began mapping the Red River Valley on the Prairies against the wishes of the 6,000 Metis (mixed blood Indians) who lived there. The Metis declared their own provisional government under a Metis called Louis Riel. The rebellion collapsed with the arrival of the British-Canadian Army and Louis Riel fled to Montana where he worked as a school teacher for 10 years. In 1884 traditional Metis lands in the Saskatchewan River Valley were sur-veyed by federal agents for white settlers. This led to another Metis uprising led again by Louis Riel. The Metis were defeated in June 1885. Louis Riel was tried and hanged in November 1885. A play based on the trial is acted out three times a day during the Summer months at Regina where the original trial took place.

S

Saskatchewan A province in the middle of Canada, 651,903 km² (251,634 mi²) with a population of about one million. The province is named after the Saskatchewan River and the name is a Cree word meaning 'river that turns around when it runs'. The province produces two thirds of Canada's wheat. The capital is Regina (see Pile o' Bones). Many of the people are Metis — of mixed Indian and European blood.

Size Canada covers nearly 10 million km² (3.9 million mi²). It is the world's second largest country after the Soviet Union.

T

Totem poles The totem pole is an ancient form of Northwest Coast Indian art. The carvings tell the stories of the Indians' ancestors. The tallest totem pole in the world is 54 m (178 ft).

U

Urbanization More than 70% of the population live in cities.

V

Vancouver Nearly half of the population of British Columbia live in Vancouver, Canada's third largest city. The city is named after Captain George Vancouver, a British explorer, who sailed there in 1792. The city is now very cosmopolitan with people coming from many ethnic backgrounds.

Vikings The Vikings are believed to have reached Canada in AD 1000. They established a settlement at what is now L'Anse-au-Meadows, Newfoundland.

Visas US, British, Australian, most European and Hong Kong citizens do not need visas for stays of up to 90 days. Visas can be extended by applying to the immigration authorities.

W

White Pass and Yukon Railway One of the world's last operating narrow-gauge railways. It was built between 1898 and 1900 to take prospectors to the new gold mines, but by the time it was complete the gold rush was over.

Y

Yukon The northernmost region of Canada, Yukon is very sparsely populated, very cold and unhospitable. During the summer, daylight lasts for 20 hours per day. The territory is double the size of the British Isles and being very mountainous much of it is still unexplored. The rich soil supports an abundance of flora and fauna. Animals you can see here include moose, caribou and grizzly bears.

INDEX